Sales Make

50 Tips To Grow Your Sales

Pat Lynch

Printed by City Print in Cork, Ireland

First Printing, 2015

ISBN: 978-0-9934694-0-4

Book design by: Orlagh O'Brien

I dedicate this book to all the amazing staff and customers who have supported me during my lifetime in business. In particular, the staff who, on short notice, dropped everything to support our clients and fulfil a customer need.

I am eternally grateful to you all for the sacrifices you made, time and time again, in the interests of our customers.

Sincere thanks to the team that helped me produce this book, including: Orlagh O'Brien, an amazing lady who oversaw the creative direction and book design; Eleanor Reilly of Think Visual, who has done a fantastic job on the book's illustrations; and Maria Rolston, for her patience and skill editing and polishing my words.

A special mention to my three wonderful daughters, Emma, Ciara and Stephanie, who gave me all the encouragement I needed to document my thoughts and complete this book.

Acknowledgements

Tips 1 – 15

TIPS 16—34

Tips 35–50

Foreword

BY

William Fitzgerald

Pat's simple but effective sales tips have been the cornerstone of his business success. They were put into action as he single-handedly acquired client after client for his award-winning company, Microtech Cleanroom Services.

His insights are a must for anyone in business or sales.

Pat shows passion in everything he does. He demonstrates amazing people skills and is both an influential and respected leader. It is a pleasure to call him my mentor, my colleague and my friend.

INTRODUCTION

BY

PAT LYNCH

Having reached the young age of 60, I realised that most of my working life is well behind me. I also realised that I have accumulated a huge amount of knowledge and experience of business and sales over the last 40 years. It is time to share this knowledge and information with the world at large.

During my time as founder and CEO of Microtech Cleanroom Services, I signed up one new client every month including many U.S multinationals. This was an exceptional achievement, if I may say so myself, and I had some of the top companies in the world as clients.

In this book, I share some of the simple yet effective tips on how I accomplished this. For anyone in business or sales, Sales Make contains many easy to action points for success.

Use the very simple sheets at the rear of the book to put your plans in place. Without plans, you will not succeed. Remember, what you focus on will happen.

Just start by putting one tip from this book into action today. Before you know it you will see the effects. Feel free to contact me with your success stories in the future.

Enjoy the book.

Sales is all about fixing problems for your customers:

ONCE YOU UNDERSTAND THIS, YOU WILL BE SUCCESSFUL.

WHAT PROBLEM ARE YOU FIXING?

Sales is all about fixing problems for your customers.
You need to know what the problem is. The problem you
think you are fixing may not be your customer's problem,
so dig deep to understand the customer's concern.
The customer will then pay you a fee for the solution or
product you are supplying. The bigger the problem, the
bigger the fee to you. Once you understand this, you will
be successful.

TELL YOUR STORY

Become a storyteller and be able to tell your story as simply as possible. Tell your client stories about how you saved costs for other customers or clients. Be able to explain your product or service as simply as possible. Perhaps have case studies to show your amazing offering and how other clients benefited from it. Be able to show a return on investment (ROI) showing the payback, if they buy your product. The faster the payback the more likely they will be to buy your product.

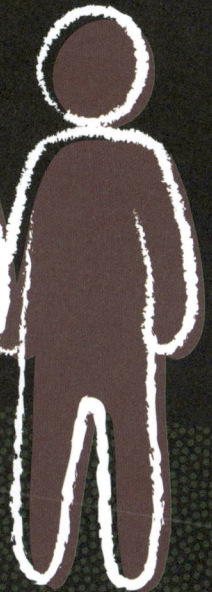

VISIT YOUR CUSTOMER

Visit your customer if possible. Whether you can afford to do this will depend on your deal size. It amazes me that so many sales people do not visit potential clients. Customers look at you differently if you make the effort to visit them. It helps you build friendships and trust. You will always get the inside story with face-to-face meetings. Bring your CEO with you to final meetings to get the deal over the line. Customers love this. Ask customers to visit you at your office or factory. They will get a much better understanding of your business issues and concerns. Take them out to lunch as part of the visit, particularly if they have travelled to your office. Try it – you will see that it works.

Find a Champion

It is important to find a champion in your client's organisation. It is vital to build a relationship with this person. They will become your internal sales person. This person will have to be your friend. Figure out what you can do for this person to make their job easier and make them look good within their business. Ideally, have several champions within your customer's company in case one leaves, becomes ill or retires. Having several means you cut down the risk of losing the client.

LISTEN TO FEEDBACK

Listen to what your customer is saying. It is amazing how many people do not listen. Their feedback can be very helpful to you as it may also apply to other customers. Make sure you document the feedback and act on it if need be. You will often see an improvement that you can make to your product or service. This can have a dramatic effect and could increase your organisation's overall sales. More importantly, it could have the effect of increasing profitability for your company.

GATHER THEIR GOOD WORDS

It is important to gather references, quotes and testimonials from clients. They may not be prepared to give them to you but if you get them, they can be worth their weight in gold. Good references are key to getting new business. It is important to know that your client will give you a good reference, either written or oral. A good reference will come from your champion in your client's organisation. Make sure you thank them for it.

Gather quotes as you go from meeting to meeting with clients. You can use them in marketing material or with other clients. Testimonials are also great to have on your website and marketing material. Always get the client's approval to use quotes etc. as not all companies will allow you to use information like this.

LISTEN AT MEETINGS

Listen rather than talk at customer meetings. At the start of a meeting, find out the titles of the people attending. Collect business cards if possible. Are they the decision makers? Ask questions at the start of the meeting to understand what the client's biggest problem is. Once you have gathered this information, you can then focus your conversation and presentation on providing a solution for that problem. Keep asking questions, listen carefully to the answers being given by the client and take notes. Listening carefully and being able to read the signals being given by the client is an art. The reason we have two ears and one mouth is to listen more and talk less.

A Free Trial?

Consider giving a free trial for a period of time. This works well if you are selling software. Make sure the trial ends after a set period of say, 30 days. Work with the client to make sure they use the product during the free trial as this helps to get them paying at the end of the trial. If you're selling a product, consider offering sample products. You may be able to afford to do this if your margins are good. Try sampling your product directly to the public in stores, with special offers if the product gets bought on the same day. Think about your business and how this might work for you.

Contact a Customer Each Day

Phone an existing customer or potential new one each day. You will be amazed how this will generate new sales. You will always find that some of your clients need extra product when you call and you will get the order. You may not get an answer when you call initially but do leave a message on their phone. They may just call you back the following week.

It is more difficult making cold calls to potential clients. You have to make many calls to get results. Always remember, one call is not enough so keep calling. If you get through to the right person just try and arrange a meeting. You can sell when you get in front of them.

WHAT KEEPS THEM UP AT NIGHT?

Have deep conversations with your client to establish what is keeping them up at night. This is not easy. What they tell you first may not be the true story. They may be reluctant to tell you. This is why you need to build strong relationships with your clients to get them to open up to you. I call this 'peeling back the onion'. Your competitors will not take the time to do this. You might consider a workshop with your client to understand their deep issues. This is what true partners do. Once you know the deep issues, you can come up with solutions.

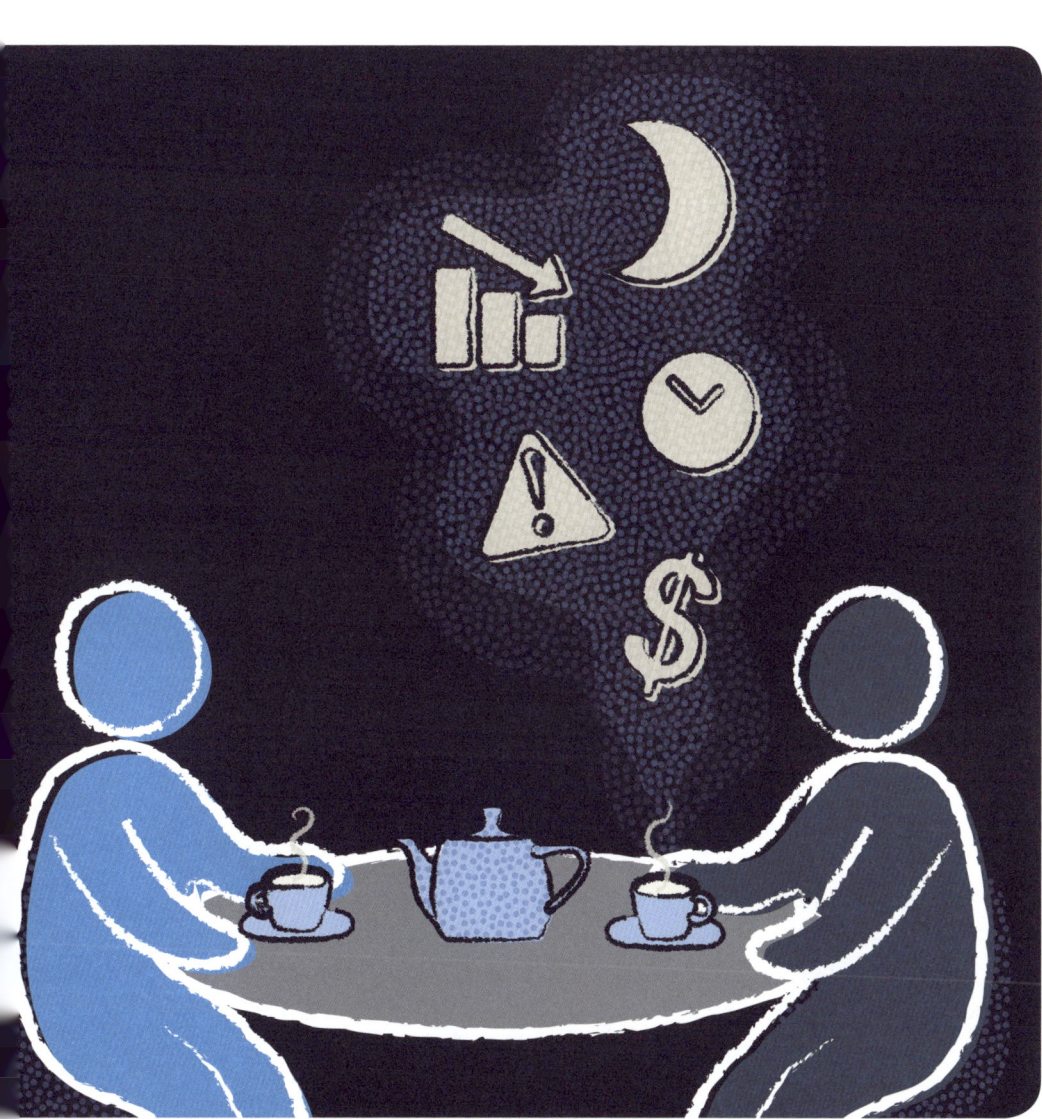

OFFER COST SAVING IDEAS

As a sales person, you are knowledgeable of the business you are in. You are learning from all of your customers and your competitors. You are like a consultant. Be careful that customers do not bleed you for ideas and then fail to give you the business. Look for ways to offer your client solutions that will help them save costs. Perhaps it might be a more frequent delivery so that they do not have to stock as much inventory. Another possibility may be using sea freight instead of air freight. It could be using cardboard instead of plastic packaging. It may be changing from paper delivery to online delivery. You are the expert, you figure it out. A good brainstorming session with your fellow colleagues will produce lots of ideas.

ALLOW YOURSELF TIME

Allow yourself time – you will need it. Remember, one phone call to a client is never enough. You need to keep following up, even if you get a "no" the first time. Know the average time span to close a deal. It may take years, depending on your business. During this time, have the patience to work with the customer to keep bringing them along, month by month, until you finally get that hard earned purchase order. During this process always ask the question, "What is the next step?" Keep building the relationship with the client over the timeframe. What a great feeling it is to close the deal!

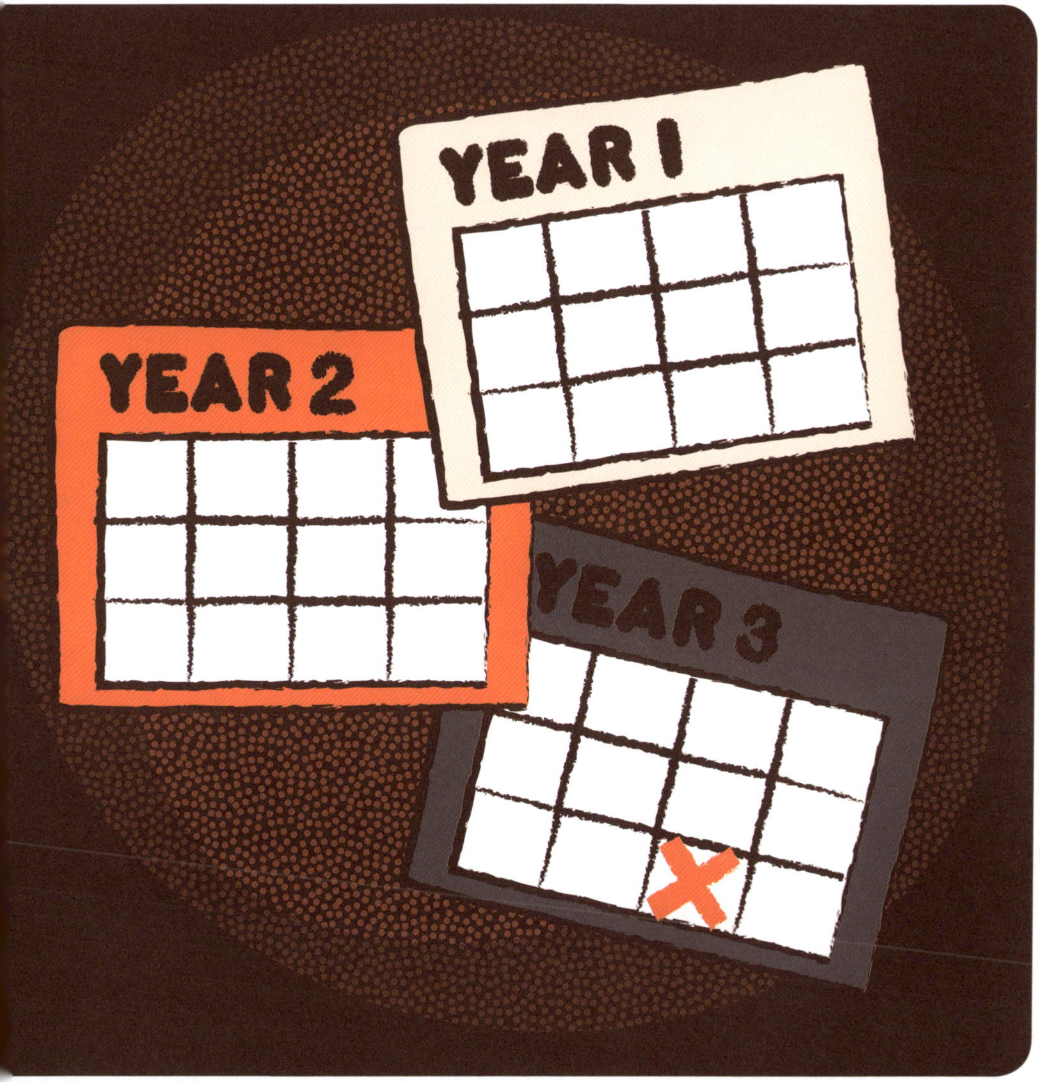
YEAR 1
YEAR 2
YEAR 3

Know The 80/20 Rule

Eighty percent of sales normally come from twenty percent of your customers. You need to know the twenty percent. Keep close to these customers. Build strong relationships with them. Visit them regularly. It is best to know who your biggest customers are each month. Know what products they are buying. Will the trend continue with these customers? Know what the margin or profit is on each of these clients.

On the other side, you need to understand the eighty percent. Are any of these customers taking up a lot of your company's time? Should you cut them loose and would you be better off without them? This is information well worth spending time analysing.

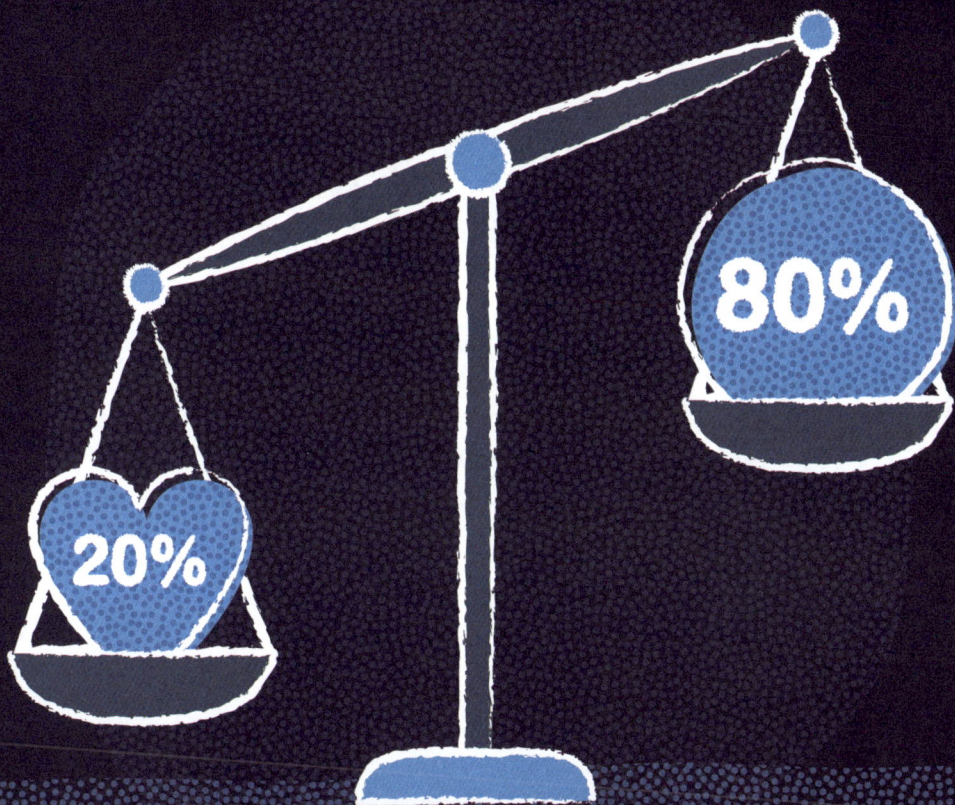

UP SELL CROSS SELL TOP DOWN SELL

When you start selling your product or services to a new client, you need to learn to up-sell other products or services to the same customer. You also need to cross-sell to other departments or sister companies in the same company or organisation. Doing both of these things will help you get more sales from the existing company. So figure out a plan to do this. Start by taking a sample of say, 5 or 10 clients and work on it. What you focus on will happen. You will see.

Selling from the top down is vital. If you can talk to decision makers you have a much better chance of making the sale. The further up the ladder in the organisation, the better chance you have of success.

GROW CHEERLEADER NETWORKS

It takes time to build support for your company's product or services within your client's organisation. Having one person supporting you is never enough. You will need several supporters within your client's company. When they need a product or service, you should be the first person they think of. During their coffee breaks, they should be discussing the fantastic service you provide. You should have so many supporters within your client's organisation that when they hit a new problem, they contact you first and you solve the problem for them. It takes years to build this relationship, so start today and put a plan in place.

HELP YOUR CLIENT AVOID LAND MINES

You must become an expert in the area that you sell in. Build your knowledge by going to shows, researching on the internet, reading white papers, etc. You should be aware of any changes coming down the tracks that may affect your clients. Let me give you a few examples: you might know about a new regulation due out in a year that will restrict your clients from using a certain type of material in their product, or you may have heard of a new market entrant operating in your client's space. Knowledge is powerful so use it strategically to your advantage. Your client will value it.

SHARE INVALUABLE KNOWLEDGE

This builds on the last point. Increase your market knowledge and know about your client's competitors. Read your client's annual reports. You will gather a wealth of information from them. Set up alerts on the internet so that when press releases are issued about any of your clients, you will receive them. Be willing to forward these press releases to your clients by email to ensure that they saw them and just say, "I thought you might be interested in these". As a result, you will become the fact gatherer for customers. You become their eyes and ears. Any time you want to visit them, you will be well received.

A CLEAR DIFFERENCE

Analyse your offering with that of all your competitors. Illustrate it on one page. It should clearly show that you offer extra features or offerings that your competitors do not. It is worth spending time on this as it can help the client make a faster decision regarding why they should go with you. This will mean that you have to do a deep dive on your competitors to fully understand what they offer versus what you offer. If you lose a deal for any reason, ask the client why they went with one of your competitors. It can be very enlightening.

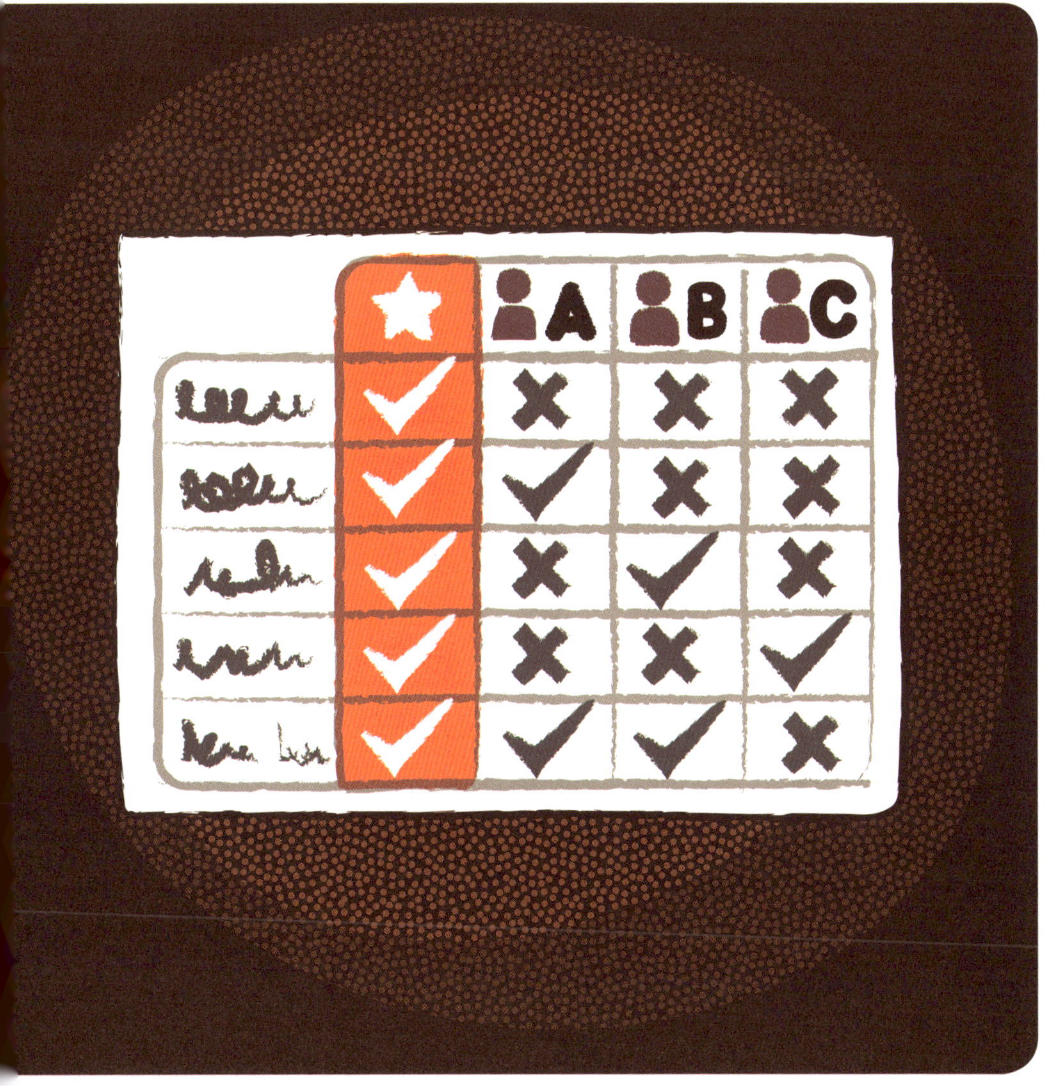
A
B
C

RESPOND QUICKLY

It is vital to respond fast to customers. If they asked for a quote, there is a good chance they want your product or service soon. You can respond via email on the same day. When one does not respond quickly it suggests that your company is non-responsive and the client may believe the same could apply to after care service. If it takes a while to put a quote together, then keep the client informed. Always let them know exactly when they will receive the quote or information that they require. Always follow up after the quote is submitted, to ensure they received it and that everything is to their satisfaction. Ask for feedback and establish when you are likely to get a decision from them.

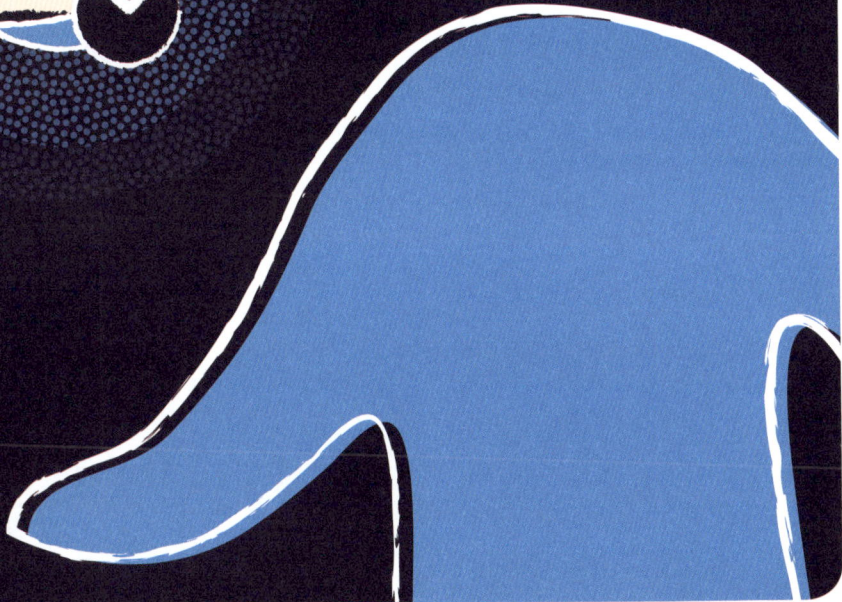

ACCEPT ANY WORK FOR STARTERS

It may sound like an inconvenience but take any work you can to get going with your client. It may be a day's consulting work or supplying a product that you do not make money on but it means you can start building a relationship with your client as a trusted supplier. What it also means is that you get set up as an approved supplier on your client's books. When the real work comes, it means you can move ahead with the supply of goods or services that bit quicker. The more services your client buys from you, the more they will depend on you.

NEVER KNOCK THE COMPETITORS

It is important that you never knock the competitors. Always say how much respect you have for them. It is best to say that you have a good healthy relationship with them. What is important is that you show how you are different from them. Perhaps you are nimbler than they are and you can react faster. Perhaps you are stronger financially. It could be that you offer your client a proper back-up service. It is worth spending time with your management, figuring out exactly what to say when you are asked about your competitors.

Help to Consider Alternatives

As a sales person you will be out and about a lot.
You have the capability of gathering lots of additional
information that's not specifically related to your
business but that can help your customers. If you share
these nuggets with your customers you can help them
a lot and you will build a great reputation. In the long
term, it will help you keep your customer because they
will appreciate the new ideas that you bring them. Some
examples include suggesting: a cheaper way for recruiting
staff; a cheaper way to transfer funds abroad where you
do not pay fees; ideas on how to limit currency exposure;
a better way for transporting your customer's product.
I am sure you will come up with your own list.

GENERATE RECURRING INCOME

Recurring income is much better than once off sales. Recurring income means that the client keeps buying the same goods or service month after month and you can have a client for years. Recurring income is very popular in the software industry and it is known as Software As A Service (SAAS). It can take a long time to secure a client but once they are on board you can have them for life. Clients that generate recurring income are a lot more valuable than those that deliver a once off sale of the product or service. With recurring sales, you normally get increased income year on year.

BUILD AN ENGAGING WEBSITE

You must have a great website and keep it updated on a regular basis – daily if need be. It is the first thing that people will look at after they meet you. You might impress the client but the website can let you down. Make sure your website is interesting enough so that people want to visit it. Put current topics on it that relate to your clients. Have interesting free information on it that potential customers will want to access. Ensure that they have to leave their full details to get access to say, a white paper written by one of your experts. These details are all leads for you to follow up on. Follow up quickly after the information is downloaded. Ask if they got benefit from the information. It can be the first conversation towards closing a deal.

HAVE GOOD MARKETING MATERIAL

It is important to have good marketing material. That means up-to-date material on your company, products and services. Get a designer to create your corporate literature. It will cost, but it is very necessary. Have pictures, charts and graphs in the design if you can. A picture tells a thousand words. Also consider using some of the traditional marketing giveaways for shows like mugs, umbrellas, USB keys etc.

ALWAYS LOOK + ACT PROFESSIONAL

It is important to look the part when you attend meetings. Dress appropriately for the meeting you are asked to attend. You may have to research the dress code of the client you are about to visit. If there is a casual dress code, then you should dress accordingly. Smart casual may be just right. If you are going to a formal meeting where you know the client will be well dressed, then you should wear a tie if you are a man or a professional suit if you are a woman. Make sure you know how to behave at client dinners or lunches. Do not drink excessively. It can be the reason why you do not get the order. If you have to fly to a meeting and there is a time zone difference, then consider flying a day early to get over the jet lag.

LISTEN RATHER THAN TALK AT CUSTOMER MEETINGS...

THE REASON WE HAVE TWO EARS IS TO LISTEN MORE AND TALK LESS.

ATTEND SHOWS +
CONFERENCES

Attend your industry shows or business conferences.
It is important to plan what shows you need to attend
in advance as your company may need to book a stand
at the events. The cost of these shows also needs to be
approved in the annual budget.

Book flights and hotels well in advance to get the best
price. Research before the shows to establish who will
be attending and who you would like to meet. Send out
emails to set up meetings with the people you want to
engage with. Make sure you have plenty of marketing
material and business cards with you. After the show,
follow up with all the leads you acquired. They can be
your pipeline for the year.

NETWORK NETWORK + NETWORK

You can never do enough networking. It is a great way to get referrals or introductions to people that you can do business with.

Always arrive early and leave late at networking events. This is the time that most of your new contacts will be made. When you meet someone at a networking event, you should focus entirely on them for the time you are talking to them – let there be no distractions. Find out what you can do for them. Give them your business card and take his/hers if they offer it. Connect with them on LinkedIn after the meeting or at latest, the next day. If they connect with you, then send them a thank you message through LinkedIn. If you think you can do business together, meet up for a coffee to talk, if possible.

A Special Deal for Customer No.1

This is a great way to get started with a new client or if you have just started a new business. It is a way to prove yourself and get a foot hold with the client. The deal may be a loss leader but it may lead to a bigger order in time. It is important that the client knows they are getting a special offer. In return you should look for a reference or testimonial from them or a promise that they will take calls from your potential clients in the future. You will also get the experience of finding out how you can solve the customer's problem. Once you get established, you will be able to go to normal pricing in time.

REWARD LOYALTY

Would a loyalty scheme work for your business?
Understand the benefits of having one. Weigh up the
cost of the extra sales versus the cost of the scheme
to you. Would a loyalty scheme bring you in new repeat
customers that would not have come to you otherwise?
What would be the effects on your overall margin? Lots
of good companies out there are offering a full loyalty
scheme package. Check them out on the internet.

GET REFERRALS FROM CUSTOMERS

This is important for growing your business. You will need to get references for your website and more importantly, be able to give potential clients the names of some existing clients that they can contact for a reference. Make sure that the clients you give as referees will in fact give you an excellent reference. Inform the clients who are to act as your referee that they should expect a call from your new potential customer. Fill them in on how your new client wants to use your product or service. Ask them to tell your possible new client how they benefited from your product or service. Perhaps they can give details of ROI (Return On Investment) and payback for their investment. That would be very beneficial to you.

Use Webinars

Webinars are a great way to talk to all your customers at the same time, including potential customers. Pick topics of interest to your industry and find experts in your field that can deliver the content. No need to do a hard sell on webinars but keep a full list of all those on the call and follow up with them afterwards by phone. If possible, use LinkedIn, LinkedIn groups and leads from shows etc. to publicise your webinars and create a schedule on your website of future webinars. Do not allow your competitors to join your webinars. No need to educate them.

WORK AT THE CLIENT'S PREMISES

This is a great way to get sticky with your client and it is becoming very popular. Travel agents and freight forwarders are using it all the time for their larger clients. They get their own office on the client's premises. Think about how you can create this scenario with your clients for the product or service that you supply. Consider doing it on a part time basis i.e. two days a week or just mornings. Clients do appreciate it. It is also harder to dislodge you once you are on site.

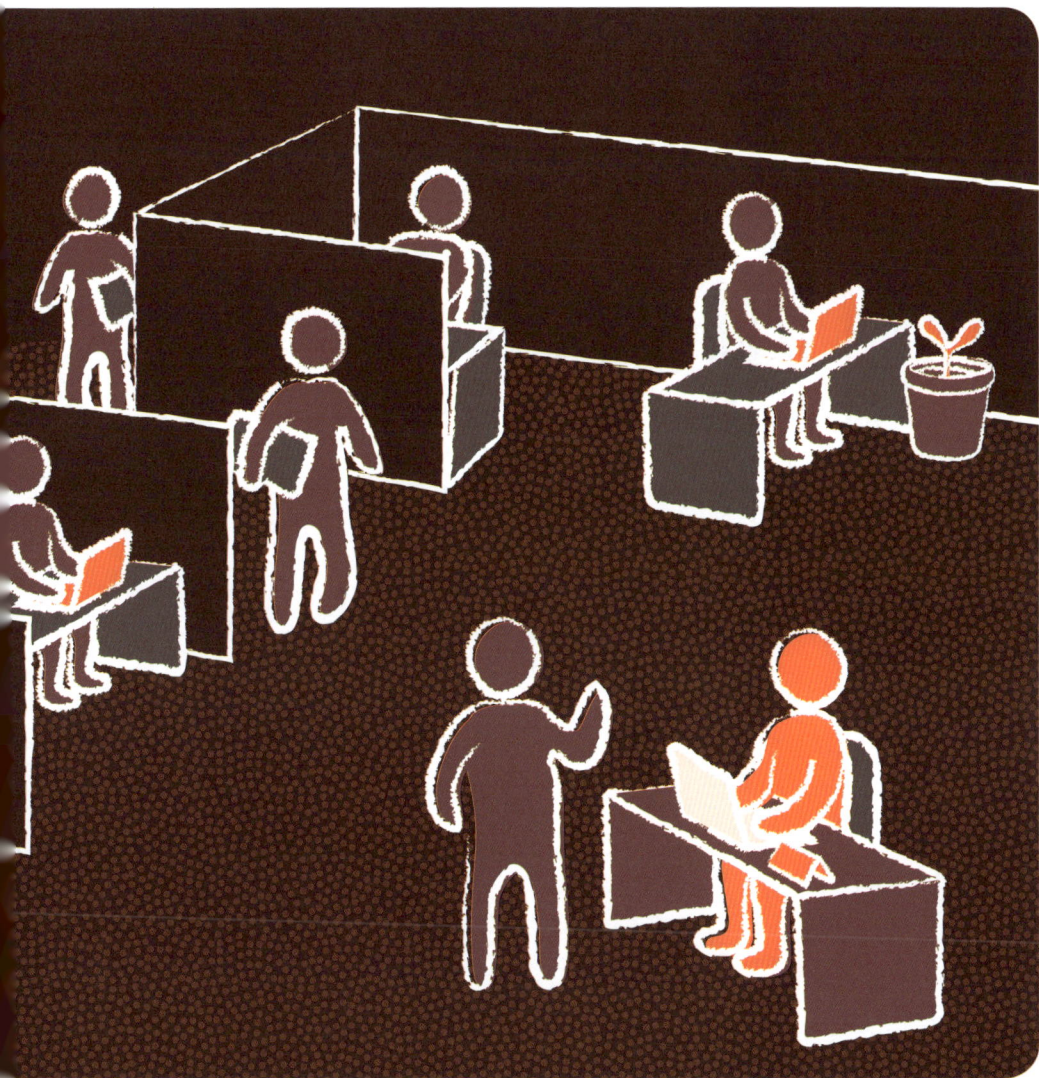

Setup the Right CRM System

A good Customer Relationship Management (CRM) system is a must to keep track of where you are in the process with all your potential and existing clients. You need all your staff to keep it up to date as they talk to customers and potential customers. There is nothing worse than two sales people contacting a potential client on the same matter. It would make you look silly. There are many CRM systems that can be bought off the shelf. It is worth spending time to find the right one to fit your needs.

Find Partners or Resellers

This can be a great way to grow if you can find the right partners or agents. Finding them is the problem. There are companies that find partners who suit your business. It is worth exploring this option. Companies often think that once your partner is found, all your sales problems are solved. This is not the case. You have to work very closely with partners to educate them on your service or product. Be prepared to meet their clients with them to explain your offering. No one will sell your product or service better than you. If you are not at these meetings, you will never know what product or service your partner is pushing.

Use Social Media

This can be a game changer if you know what you are doing. Try to educate your audience through your social media rather than sell to them. It will gain much better traction from your audience. For example, if you are a travel agent, what will get more traction – offers on cruises or 20 tips on how to enjoy your cruise? Education through social media will generate much better results in the line of long term sales. Also consider starting a blog, it's a great way to build loyalty.

OFFER GLOBAL Solutions

If you want to grow value in your business then you have to think globally and offer global solutions. Know which countries your clients operate out of and see if there is some way you can offer the same solution globally rather than just supplying the local market. It will help you grow quickly. Think about how you can offer a better solution to fix your customer's problem. Perhaps it might be dropping your product to their production line three times a day to meet their demand. You will need to work with your customers to figure this out and your customer will need to be happy with you as a service provider.

Build close relationships with your clients...

ONCE YOU KNOW
THE DEEP ISSUES
YOU CAN COME
UP WITH
SOLUTIONS.

TRUST, RELATIONSHIP + PERFORMANCE

Business is built on trust, relationships and performance. Your clients therefore need to have complete faith that you can deliver the service you promise them. You can have a great presentation at meetings but remember, if you get the business, you have to deliver.

Do not over promise before you get the contract. I would rather see you over deliver when the contract has been secured. The customer will be happier with that.

Make Videos

Videos are a great way to get noticed. You should have one made for your company or update your existing one. Make sure you use short videos. Most people have a short attention span. One-minute videos work well. Get someone creative to produce them for you and they will tell the story for you. Make sure your message is clear and to the point.

ACT BIGGER THAN YOU ARE

Companies do not want to do business with small companies or companies that may go out of business. When you start a business, you will possibly be small. You will need to act bigger than you are and be able to answer questions that will potentially be asked regarding your size. If you have a meeting with your client at their office, then bring as many relevant people as possible to the meeting. It may have to be your mentor or advisor but make sure you look bigger than a one man show. Talk about the people back at the office. Should your client ask to visit you at your office, make sure everyone is present that day. You will look like a much bigger organisation and it will give comfort to your client.

READ SALES BOOKS + ATTEND COURSES

Every time I read a sales book, I get a new idea.
How many sales books besides this one have you read?
It is important to keep up to date. There is an incredible
choice of books on this subject to read. Also, think about
attending seminars on sales. You can learn a lot from
networking with like-minded people. You will be surprised,
they will all have the same problem as you – how to get
more sales.

Be Passionate

Without passion you will not succeed. The buyer
needs to hear the excitement in your voice. You must
love Mondays, the start of a new week, and feel excited
about how you can make a difference. Excitement
comes as a result of you knowing how you can fix the
customer's problem and the customer being excited
about proceeding with you. Customers love to meet
sales people who have passion.

PEOPLE BUY FROM PEOPLE

At the end of the day, people buy from people and not from companies. Every day, I see that people buy products and services that they do not really want, from people that they like and trust. I also see people with a need or requirement who defer the buying decision because they really do not like the person selling the product or service. Think about the sales people that call to see you. You will always meet the people that you like.

HAVE A SALES PLAN

The overall company needs to have a sales plan. Each sales person needs to have their own individual portion of this plan. The plan needs to be broken down into quarters and months. Each month, the sales made must be measured against the plan. The sales person needs to know how they will fulfil their plan each month, both by customer and product. The company needs to understand the profit margin by customer and product to ensure that the overall profit target for the company will be met for the year.

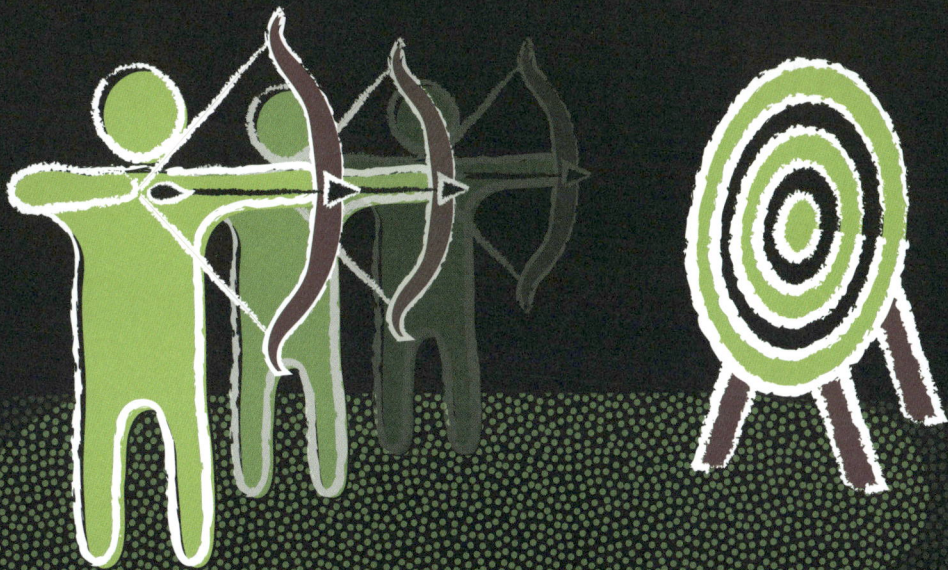

QUALIFY YOUR CLIENTS

Getting a RFQ (Request For Quote) does not mean you will get the business. The client may be looking for quotes but they know who they will give the business to. When you are dealing with a client, it is always important that they have the budget and the decision making power to go ahead and place the order with you. Make sure that you are dealing with the right person within the organisation, otherwise you are wasting a lot of time.

One Call is Never Enough

Some deals take a long time to close. Make sure you have the patience and money to close large deals that could take many years to obtain. One phone call to clients is never enough to get the business. In fact, if you make 100 cold calls, you may only get one or two clients that are interested in talking to you. So your sales funnel must be filled by lots of calls resulting in interest, resulting in quotations which could finally result in a sale.

Be Interested in People

This rule has already been mentioned in this book but is worth saying again. Certain people have a personality for sales. It is usually people who get on well with people. They usually know how to open up conversations, talk about the weather or even talk about the match at the weekend. I know one sales person who looks up the potential client's Facebook page to find out their hobbies. He will always try to bring the conversation to their interests and it works.

UNDER PROMISE
OVER DELIVER

This is so important. Many sales people over promise before they get the order. They sell their souls to get the deal. This is not a good way to behave. Their company then appears to be under delivering when the service or product is to be supplied. It is much better to be seen to be over delivering when you start with the client. You will be much more likely to get more orders from the client when you over deliver.

Post
Thank You Cards

This is a novel idea. We have stopped using the traditional postman. It is so nice to receive a card in the post, thanking you for the business or the referral. It is much better than an email. Customers remember these small gestures. So go and get a box of cards and have them in your drawer. Start writing the cards when you need them. It will show that you are a genuine person.

ASK FOR THE BUSINESS

Sales people do everything except ask for the business. Do not be afraid to make that call with the sole purpose of saying that you are asking for the client's business. You will have your reasons e.g. "The board meets next week," or that you need to fill your monthly sales target. If you call 10 customers, you should surely get some orders.

PHONE AN EXISTING CUSTOMER OR POSSIBLE NEW ONE EACH DAY...

ONE CALL
IS NEVER
ENOUGH, SO
KEEP
TRYING.

Choose your Goal

Set your Plan

It's time to make it happen...

Take Action

CONTACT A CUSTOMER EACH DAY

MOTIVATION

MY PLAN

WHY To increase sales

COMPLETION DATE

1 Make a list of the people to call

2 Set a time to make calls each day

3 Make the call and document it in CRM system

4 Follow up on the action items from the call

5 Meet with the client if possible

6 Obtain purchase order from client

COMMITTMENT

SIGNED

DATE

USE WEBINARS

WHY To obtain more sales leads

COMPLETION
DATE

1 Choose the Webinar topic, speaker and date

2 Email existing and potential clients

3 Promote the Webinar on social media, eg. LinkedIn

4 Hold and record the Webinar

5 Follow up with the attendees

6 Arrange customer visits and close deals

7 Plan the next series of Webinars

SIGNED   DATE

NETWORK

WHY To increase sales leads

1 Select industry shows or conferences to attend

2 Obtain event budget

3 Decide who you want to meet at the events

4 Attend all selected events

5 Gather new contact leads while there

6 Follow up with new leads afterwards

SIGNED

DATE

DOODLE & DREAM

WHY

COMPLETION
DATE

1

2

3

4

5

6

SIGNED   DATE

NOTES

DOODLE & DREAM

WHY
COMPLETION
DATE

1
2
3
4
5
6

SIGNED
DATE

DOODLE & DREAM

WHY

COMPLETION
DATE

1

2

3

4

5

6

SIGNED   DATE

NOTES

DOODLE & DREAM

	WHY	COMPLETION DATE
1		
2		
3		
4		
5		
6		

SIGNED .... DATE ....

Coming Soon:

Business Make

Pat's Fifty Tips